Great Yarmouth Row Houses
and Greyfriars' Cloister

Bronwen Riley

Introduction

The inhabitants of Great Yarmouth liked to boast that, like some legendary city, their town 'rose out of the sea' – and in a sense it had, for it was founded on a sand spit squeezed between the river Yare and the North Sea. Within these watery confines lay the town's famously narrow lanes, or rows. They are first mentioned in the 1280s, and most of the 145 rows survived until bombs and town planners did away with them in the mid-20th century.

As a flourishing port grown fat on its trade in herring, Yarmouth was attractive to orders of friars such as the Franciscans, known as the grey friars, who relied on donations for their income. They arrived here in the 13th century and their church and conventual buildings occupied a large area in the centre of town. After the friary's suppression in 1538 the property was sold off and converted into houses, including the part of the cloister that survives today.

The two row houses now, like Greyfriars' Cloister, in the care of English Heritage, were built in the early 17th century. Known as Row 111 House and the Old Merchant's House, they were the homes of confident merchants – men content to live where they worked, among their shops and smokehouses and within sight of their ships. Both houses were altered in the 18th century to keep up with changing fashions, but thereafter their status declined as they were let out to multiple tenants. With rare plasterwork ceilings and an outstanding collection of artefacts from demolished houses, they now offer a tantalizing glimpse into the lost world of the rows.

Tour

The tour begins at Row 111 House, where many architectural fixtures and fittings rescued after the Second World War from now demolished row houses are on display. The exhibition continues at the Old Merchant's House, which also contains two exuberant early 17th-century plasterwork ceilings.

At Greyfriars' Cloister, visitors can see the only remains in England of the cloister of a Franciscan friary, together with a rare wall-painting discovered in the south aisle of the friary church.

FOLLOWING THE TOUR

This section provides tours of Row 111 House (starting on page 5), the Old Merchant's House (page 12) and Greyfriars' Cloister (page 20). Greyfriars' Cloister is open by guided tour only, by arrangement with the custodian of the two row houses. The numbers beside the headings highlight key points in the tour and correspond with the small numbered plans in the margins.

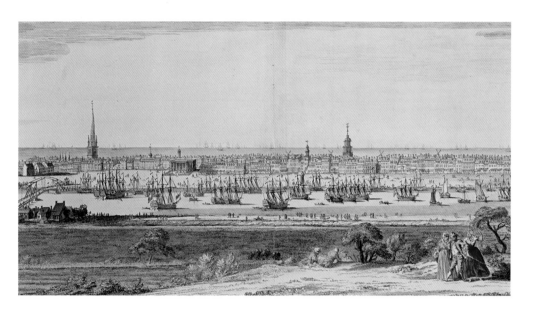

THE LOST ROWS

The two row houses are now isolated in a sea of post-war development that disregards the old street pattern. Today, the visitor can look from one building to the other across an open space, yet, until the area was heavily bombed during the Second World War, the two houses stood in narrow rows crammed with buildings, with another row, Row 112, between them.

The town's 145 rows were built east to west down to the river Yare. Some of the grandest houses in town stood on the spacious and much admired Quay and the two row houses were situated in prime locations, set just back from it. When they were built in the early 17th century, their main entrances faced the Quay. Access to and from the river would have been important for the merchants who lived here. They would have been able to watch their ships in the harbour from the upper rooms of their properties. Daniel Defoe, who visited the town in 1722, described how the ships rode so close together with their bows touching the wharf that you could walk from ship to ship, as though on a gigantic floating bridge.

Above: Detail of an engraving of Great Yarmouth from the west by Nathaniel and Samuel Buck, 1741. The Row 111 House and Old Merchant's House were set just back from the Quay

Below: Row 111 House in 1949, after being badly damaged during the Second World War

Facing page: Decorative 17th-century panelling on a door found after the war at No. 9 Row 117, the eastern part of the Old Merchant's House

ROW 111 HOUSE

Badly bombed during the Second World War, this house was saved from demolition because its 17th-century structure remained largely intact. It was restored during the 1950s with the intention of revealing as much of its original form as possible. No documentation regarding the house survives and we do not know whether it was occupied in the 17th-century as one, two or even three dwellings. By the outbreak of the Second World War the house had been divided into three (Nos 6, 7 and 8) and was home to the Lee, Hook and Rainer families. At this time, outhouses containing privies, coppers (water-heaters) and pigeons filled the yards, and warehouses and malthouses surrounded the house. The smell of fish pervaded everywhere.

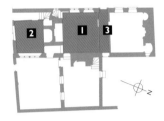

1 2 Kitchen and Shop

The room which now contains the shop and ticket office may, in the 17th century, have been the kitchen of the double-fronted house facing the Quay. In an arrangement typical of Yarmouth houses, the staircase beside the huge chimney-stack leads to the chamber above.

The room to the south, which faces the row and is now a cafe, may well have been in a different occupancy or used as a shop. The way in which the Row III House may have been split is suggested by the arrangement made in the will of William Cosh, a bailiff of the town who died in 1681. He left his house to his nephews, on condition that his wife should be allowed 'to have solely to her own proper use, the kitchen of the said dwelling-house, and the chamber over the same, and the garrett over the said chamber; and also jointly … the use and benefit of the washhouse and washhouse chamber, pump and yards'.

The cafe has an 18th-century fireplace, though the large chimney-stack is 17th-century. The window overlooking the yard is a replica of a 17th-century four-light window; its central carved mullion is original. This southern unit of the house was given a new brick gable in the 19th century with its own entrance front, sash windows and staircase; it is not clear what arrangement this replaced. The short passageway next to the chimney-stack was blocked off when the house was divided.

3 Cross-passage

From the 19th century until the 1940s a staircase ran from this passage to the first floor. When the house was restored after the war, panelling from 47 South Quay, now demolished, was installed here. The position of the back door was moved slightly north when the east range was added in the 1630s.

Right: Row houses had wells and pumps in the courtyards, often shared between neighbours. This painting of 1657 by the Dutch artist Pieter de Hooch shows women washing clothes in a Delft courtyard

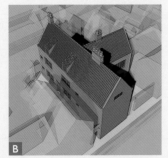

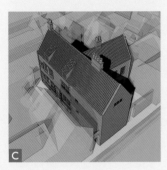

The development of
Row III House

A about 1600: the main entrance
fronts the Quay to the west

B about 1630: an east wing is
added, giving the building
a T-shaped plan

C about 1680: the entrance front
is given new windows and faced
in brick and flint

D about 1900: the house now has
sash windows and the southern
unit has its own entrance front
facing onto Row III

How the House Changed

The best place to gain a sense of how the Row III House may
have looked when it was built in the early 17th century, and
how it changed over time, is outside its west facade, the original
entrance front facing the Quay. The original house (A) had a
spacious room on either side of the entrance door (which now
has an 18th-century surround). This opened onto a passage
running the breadth of the house. There were two rooms on
the first floor and a garret above. Each of the four rooms was lit
by a four-light window (the lintels survive *in situ*) and heated by
a fireplace. A staircase ran up one side of each chimney-stack.
Small windows, seen to the right, lit the stairs; the tiny first-floor
window to the left lights a closet, or small room. A further unit,
one-room deep, extended south onto the row. This may have
been used as a shop or been in a different occupancy.

In about 1630 (B) an east wing, one room deep over
three floors, was added to the house. It was connected to the
southern unit by diagonal passages on the ground and first
floors – the south and east units perhaps formed a separate unit.

In about 1680 (C) windows on the entrance front were
replaced with two-light windows, and a brick and knapped
flint facing was added, which does not extend to the southern
bay, nor to the small stackside windows to the south (right).
This breaks the symmetry of the double front, making it look
cramped, and suggests that at the time it was added another
building abutted the south-west side of the house. It also
reaffirms the likelihood that the southern unit was separate.

By about 1900 (D), the house had been divided into three
and the southern unit had its own entrance from the row.

*Below: The original entrance front
(right) and the yard wall, which was
rebuilt in the 1950s to show the
distinctive patterns of brickwork once
found in the rows*

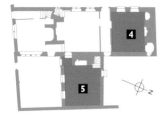

4 Hall/Parlour

In the 17th century this room was probably described as a hall and used as a reception room and a place to dine. A staircase running up the side of the chimney, which was later removed and replaced with a cupboard, led to the chamber above. In the 18th century sash windows were inserted and the room was newly panelled. The inbuilt buffet, to the left of the fireplace, would have been used to display silver and china. The fireplace tiles depicting sea monsters, ships and mermaids represent suitably marine themes for a house in Yarmouth and were rescued from other row properties. Although many surviving delftware tiles in England were in fact made in London and Liverpool, it seems likely that those here were made in Holland, given its strong trading and cultural links with Yarmouth. Rotterdam was a shorter sail from Yarmouth than London, and supplied the town with a huge range of goods. Note the Dutch flags on the distinctive boats.

5 East Wing

Added to the house in about 1630, this wing contained a room on each of its three floors (ground and first floors and attic) and a small cellar. Its chimney-stack backed onto the wall of the original house. Although the wing has lost most of its 17th-century features, it appears to have been of high quality. It is possible that this wing had its own entrance even in the 17th century, with a door in the same place as it is now.

To the east (left) of the back door into the wing is a blocked early 19th-century doorway. When this wing was occupied as a separate dwelling by the Lee family in the 1930s, there was a small lean-to at the back which they used as a

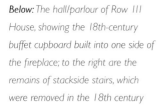

Below: The hall/parlour of Row III House, showing the 18th-century buffet cupboard built into one side of the fireplace; to the right are the remains of stackside stairs, which were removed in the 18th century

kitchen. They kept coal in the 17th-century cellar. Inside what was the Lees' living room on the ground floor, the fireplace has been exposed to reveal the 17th-century lintel. In the 19th century the fireplaces throughout the building were reduced in size when cast-iron grates were installed.

In the 1930s, the first-floor room was used as a bedroom. The diagonal passage next to the landing space would have been blocked up when the Lees lived here, as the adjoining room belonged to the Hook family in No. 7. On display here and throughout the building are items salvaged from now demolished row houses after the war (see pages 10–11).

First floor

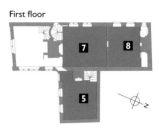

Attic

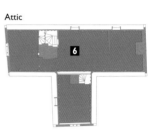

6 Attic

The roof was almost entirely rebuilt following war damage. In the 1930s the Rainer family let out their part of the attic to paying guests in the summer. Many families in the rows made extra income by renting rooms to the 'fisher girls' who came down from Scotland during the herring season to gut and pack fish (see page 38). The attic room over the east wing, now used for storage, was used as a bedroom by the Lee family.

7 8 Kitchen Chamber and Withdrawing Chamber

In the 17th century the chamber above the kitchen was reached by spiral stairs built into the side of the chimney-stack in the kitchen below. The room also had access to the attic. By contrast, the chamber above the hall/parlour was the most private in the house, with no access to the attic. The small room to the left of the fireplace here was a closet, which in the 17th century may have been used for storage (perhaps of expensive commodities), or for the close stool.

Below: The Tea Table, an engraving of about 1710. The buffet niche by the fireplace is similar to that in the hall/parlour of Row III House, displaying all the china and silver used for the fashionable pastime of tea-drinking

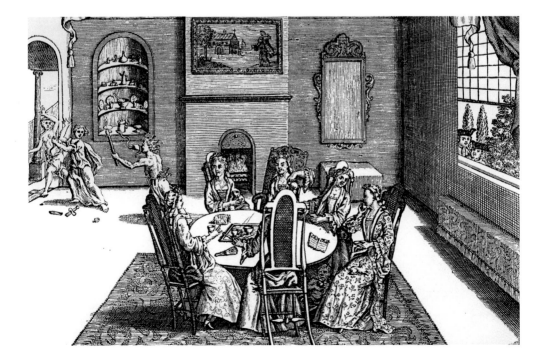

Above: Nos 6 and 7 Middlegate Street in 1945. The three spade-shaped wall anchors, or ties, seen on the facades were saved and are now on display at the Old Merchant's House

Right: Cart used to collect salvaged items from condemned row houses during and after the Second World War

Below: Victorian glazed door panel from a demolished house in Middlegate Street, and now on display in Row III House's attic

The Collection

In 1943 a team of architectural investigators headed by Bryan O'Neil began to tour the heavily bombed rows between South Quay and Middlegate Street. The weeds grew quickly and high among the bombed-out houses and a distinctive, powerful smell of damp and plaster hung in the air. The team discovered that while the bombs had blasted away gates, doors, roofs and later extensions, they had laid bare the original structures of a number of houses, revealing that many dated from the early 17th century. As O'Neil commented, it became possible, through the tragic incidence of war, to see what Yarmouth in its heyday had looked like.

It was clear that the houses, whose future before the war had already been in doubt, would not be saved. Instead, the team photographed the buildings and their fittings *in situ*. They then took away all items of interest, including doors, doorways, windows, panelling, fireplaces, hinges, wall anchors and door-knockers. Their intention was to use them to restore Row III House, the Old Merchant's House and Greyfriars' Cloister.

Many of these items are now on display at Row III House and the Old Merchant's House. Ranging in date from the 15th to 19th centuries, this architectural collection from Great Yarmouth row houses is one of the most important of its kind. At first sight, the unfurnished rooms may look empty, but they are in fact full of objects arranged around the walls.

There is a richness of detail and high standard of craftsmanship in even the most ordinary items, such as the distinctive cock's-head hinges and wall brackets. Many items reveal a delight in pattern and colour, with glass and tiles being used to maximize light – especially important in the dark and narrow row houses.

The high quality of the work from the medieval period to the 18th century reflects Great Yarmouth's wealth. The town's trading and cultural links with Holland are seen in the many examples of Dutch tiles and decorative wall anchors (a large display of which may be seen in the Old Merchant's House – see page 17).

From the late 18th century the status of the row houses declined and their poorer inhabitants recycled what they could. A medieval door in the room above the cafe was later painted and in the late 19th century two of its panels were replaced with coloured glass depicting three children playing at daisy chains. In the attic there is an early 19th-century door, with an oval panel of bull's-eye glass, made for a ship's cabin but later converted for use in a house in Middlegate Street. Another object that looks as though it came from a boat is the 19th-century figurehead of a man with moustache and sideburns in the kitchen chamber. Paint is still visible on his peaked cap and red jacket with black buttons.

Also bearing traces of red paint is the carved Tudor door-head on display in the parlour chamber. Behind it is a huge six-light window frame, which was found in a bombed-out warehouse in Row 108, which adjoins Row 111. Its central mullion is carved with an acanthus scroll and inscription bearing the date 1565.

Above: Doorpost from a demolished row house, with the appearance of a ship's figurehead, possibly dating from the 1870s
Below: Detail of Delft tiles in the hall/parlour fireplace
Bottom: Part of the collection on display on the first floor of the east wing

Right: The north facade of the Old Merchant's House, which fronted onto Row 117, looking across from Row 111. Row 112 once stood between them

Below: The Old Merchant's House just after its restoration in the early 1950s. Note the narrowness of the row

Bottom: The entrance passage, which was widened in the 18th century to accommodate the stairs

OLD MERCHANT'S HOUSE

This brick and flint house was built in the earliest years of the 17th century, a period of prosperity in Great Yarmouth. The herring shoals had returned in great numbers and many new houses were built at this time. We do not know who first lived here, but the flamboyant plasterwork ceilings and fine oak panelling indicate that it was home to a prosperous merchant of some standing in the town. Like Row 111 House, its main entrance faced the Quay to the west. In the 18th century a passage led straight from the Quay to its front door. The house had a porch and 'forechamber fronting the Quay' but it is not known if this was original. Adjoining this was a shop which also belonged to the house, and there were fish-houses, herring spits and storehouses to the east.

In the 19th century the house was divided into two tenements. The portion to the west, which later became No. 8, contained the plasterwork ceilings which were remarkable enough to be mentioned in histories and guides to the town. No. 8 was bought by Great Yarmouth Historical Buildings Company in 1908 and opened to the public. After the house was damaged in the Second World War, the Ministry of Works restored the cottage and the adjoining No. 9, creating one house again and stripping away most of the later additions.

▮ Entrance Passage

A gate in the wall (probably original) from the former Row 117 leads into a small courtyard. The house is entered through a narrow two-storey outbuilding of the late 19th or early 20th century. In the 1930s this contained a copper and a cooking range. It is possible that this outbuilding replaced an earlier structure associated with the forechamber, porch and passage mentioned in 18th-century leases. While the 17th-century door frame is original, the door once belonged to a house in Middlegate Street. A narrow passage originally gave access to the principal ground-floor chamber. This passageway was widened in the 18th century to accommodate the stairs.

2 Hall

With its splendid ceiling and patriotic royal coat of arms, this room would probably have been called the hall when first built. It may have had some public use, perhaps as the place where the merchant who owned it conducted official business or entertained business associates. Originally the room was much larger. The splendid plasterwork ceiling extended further into what are now the passageway and the adjoining room to the east: the royal coat of arms was designed as the centrepiece of the room (see feature, page 15). The handsome oak panelling is 17th-century but has clearly been altered to fit the smaller room; white paint indicates where the original panelling has been lost. The chimney-piece does not survive but would have been elaborately carved.

The room was lit originally by a long window in the west wall and a shorter five-light window in the north wall facing the street (what looks like a white painted cupboard marks its

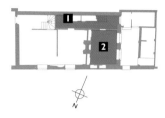

A cutaway reconstruction of the Old Merchant's House in the early 17th century

A Main entrance
B Hall
C Withdrawing chamber
D Attic
E Kitchen
F Kitchen chamber

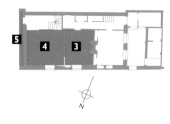

Right: Detail of the hall. The room was originally much larger – the royal coat of arms seen partially at the top left of the picture would have been the centrepiece of the room

Below: Scene in a 17th-century Dutch kitchen, by Pieter de Hooch, 1673

position). In the 17th century windows had shutters (rather than curtains), which insulated a room and also blocked out external light. Wax candles were expensive and so used sparingly, and the main source of light in a room at night would have been the fire. The white plaster ceiling would have had a brightening effect, and in the flickering light the figures in the pendants would have seemed alive.

The hall was much reduced in size in the 18th century when a new chimney-stack was inserted, dividing the room in two, and the corridor partition was moved further into the room to accommodate the stairs in the entrance passage.

3 Parlour

The parlour is the middle of three ground-floor rooms of the 18th-century house. The original house had only two rooms on each floor; the hall extended about a metre into this room, the rest of which was occupied by the huge chimney-stack that rose through the centre of the house. The curve in the wall to the right of the window indicates the position of a spiral staircase to the rooms above, reached through a door from the kitchen. In the early 18th century there may have been a buffet cupboard on one side of the fireplace, similar to the one on display.

4 5 Kitchen and Yard

The kitchen has undergone radical changes and it is now hard to imagine in its early 17th-century form, when there was a

The Plasterwork Ceilings

The plasterwork ceilings in the Old Merchant's House are remarkable survivals from the early 17th century. They can be dated fairly precisely by the royal coat of arms that once formed the centrepiece of the ground-floor room. It contains the Irish harp, which was first incorporated by James I (1603–27), together with a Latin motto which was used in the early years of his reign but thereafter dropped.

Although provincial in style, the work is of high quality: only a person of some wealth would have been able to afford it. The choice of a royal coat of arms as the centrepiece of the room suggests that whoever commissioned it held public office. A coat of arms showed loyalty to the new regime: it was placed in the room where most people would see it, rather than in the private chambers on the first floor.

The ribs are distinctive, looking rather like heftily piped-out icing sugar. This chunkiness is apparent in other ceilings from Great Yarmouth. Such a similarity in style points to the work of a regional school, although too little survives to be certain.

There is a great richness of decoration. The first-floor ceiling contains a profusion of flowers and fruit. On the ground floor, however, are some curious pendants, incorporating a winged figure with a pig's face, a pig's head and what looks like a partridge. There is a crudeness to these figures: the winged figure has the look of a ship's figurehead, and the pig, far from being a heraldic boar, has a comical aspect. Here is seaside swagger – as well as tantalizing clues, no doubt, as to the name of the owner of the house and the nature of his business.

> On the ground floor are some curious pendants, incorporating a winged figure with a pig's face, a pig's head and what looks like a partridge

Above: The winged creature with a pig's face in the hall ceiling. Its meaning is now obscure. During the 16th and early 17th centuries there was a craze for puns and hidden meanings, expressed verbally and visually

Left: The royal coat of arms in the hall ceiling, containing the Irish harp incorporated by James I. Below is the Latin motto from the opening of Psalm 68, 'exurgat deus dissipentur inimici' (Let God arise; let his enemies be scattered), which James used in the early years of his reign

First floor

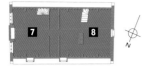

Attic

Right: The first-floor staircase looking east. The staircase was inserted in the 18th century; previously the upper floors were reached by stairs running beside the central chimney-stack

Below: A tank in the south-west corner of the cellar, which may have been used to rinse herring, or perhaps to store salt

large fireplace in its west wall. Access to the kitchen would have been via the entrance passage. The partition here was erected by the Ministry of Works after the war. A 1945 plan shows that there was a small fireplace in this location, probably dating to the 19th century.

In 1945 the yard outside the kitchen contained an outbuilding which housed a copper and adjoined the lavatory in the corner. The inhabitants did not have indoor bathrooms and would have heated water in the copper for washing. In the 18th century there was a stable on this side of the property, as well as fish-houses, where herring were cured.

Cellar

Stairs lead from the kitchen down to the cellar, where there is a large square tank in the south-west corner. It has been suggested that it was used to soak herring before they were smoked, but 18th-century documentation describes the fish-houses and vats as being to the east of the house.

6 7 Kitchen Chamber and East Attic Chamber

In the 17th century, the first-floor room above the kitchen would have been a bedchamber. A staircase built into the side of the original chimney-stack led from the kitchen straight into this room. It would have been heated by a fireplace in the west wall. The five-light window in the east wall is a copy: the

17th-century lintel above it is original. There was a similar window in the north wall – part of its lintel is visible in the recess of the wall. By 1945 the room had been divided: there was a small room at the top of the stairs with its own door and fireplace, and the larger room also had a fireplace, with an adjoining stackside cupboard.

Stairs from here lead up to the attic, which was initially two rooms divided by the central stack, but is now divided into three. The east gable has a 17th-century fireplace and window. The chimney-stack that forms a decorative feature on the outside gable served the eastern attic room alone, stopping short of the first floor.

8 Wall Anchor Display Room

This attic room had direct access from the ground floor via the stairs by the central chimney-stack, and would have been heated by a fireplace. Traces of the original window can be seen in the west gable. The present staircase was inserted when the house was divided into two in the 18th century.

The room now contains a display of wall anchors rescued from row houses after the war. Wall anchors were probably introduced to Great Yarmouth from the Low Countries. They were iron cramps, used to tie brick walls to the timber framework of a building to prevent distortion when a structure was built on an unstable surface such as sand or polder.

Although wall anchors were used elsewhere in England, Yarmouth had the largest number. They seem to have been most prevalent in the town between about 1560 and 1691, a period when many houses were built of brick following a ban on timber-framed houses. This was also a time when Dutch refugees settled here, and there were many trading links with Holland where wall anchors were in common use. Rather than providing stability, their use in Yarmouth may have been more a question of fashion: there are examples of anchors as dates, initials or fleurs-de-lis. One particularly elaborate example (see title page) takes the form of a merchant's mark.

Above: *Decorative wall anchor from a row house*
Left: *Part of the collection on display in the kitchen chamber on the first floor. The 17th-century painted door was found in No. 9 Row 117, the eastern part of the Old Merchant's House. The pattern on its panels echoes some of the decorative details found on the panelling in the withdrawing chamber*

Like many Yarmouth men Henry Lombe owned shares in ships, including the *Nancy*, the *Concord* and the *Friendship*

Who Lived in the House?

The 17th-century owners of the Old Merchant's House must for now remain nameless. Henry Lombe, who was mayor of Great Yarmouth in 1725, is its earliest recorded inhabitant. He owned a block of property on the row, including a shop fronting the Quay which he rented out to Josiah Peartree, a compass maker. This shop may have been medieval in origin: one of its rooms straddled a medieval arch across the row. The merchant's mark illustrated on page 1 was fixed to its wall. Lombe also owned fish-houses adjoining the house to the east and at least two other tenements in the town.

Like many Yarmouth men Henry Lombe owned shares in ships, including the *Nancy*, the *Concord* and the *Friendship*. In 1720 he sold property in Sunderland, where he presumably had trading links. By this date his wife had died, and he perished from smallpox in 1730. As he had no surviving children he left the bulk of his estate to his brother Samuel. A trustee of the Charity School, he also left £20 to teach poor children to read and to educate them as Christians in the Church of England.

After Samuel's death his brother's only surviving child, Elizabeth Martha, inherited the property. She lived in Gorleston with her husband John Rising, a cordwainer, and they rented the house to various people before selling it in the 1770s. By the late 18th century James Bellord, a roughmason, had acquired the whole property. He sold the former shop, by then an alehouse called the George, together with the forechamber, porch and passage, to a brewer, and built a tenement on part of the site of the fish-houses. The Bellords were the last owners to live in the house: James's nephew Samuel, a shipmaster in Ireland, inherited and in 1801 it was sold to Robert Cory (see page 37).

9 Withdrawing Chamber

This room, like the hall below it, was originally much larger, and spanned the full width of the house. It was divided into two rooms when the chimney-stack was moved in the 18th century. Two grooves cutting across the plasterwork in the corridor indicate that there was an earlier partition here. This room would have been a more private space in the 17th century, having access only from the room below.

The ceiling is richly ornamented with flowers and fruit, but unlike the room below there is no central coat of arms, nor strange figures. The focus of the room was the six-pointed star, which has lost its central pendant. The panelling is also highly decorative and when new the oak would have been much lighter. A bed with brightly coloured curtains and valences, and boldly embroidered cushions on chairs and stools, would have added to the sumptuousness of the room. Nearby Norwich was famous for its textiles.

Left: The withdrawing chamber on the first floor

Below: A mid-17th-century painting of a lady in her bedchamber, by an unknown Dutch artist. Beyond the bed is a closet with a close stool – many rooms had adjoining closets which could also be used for storage or as small studies

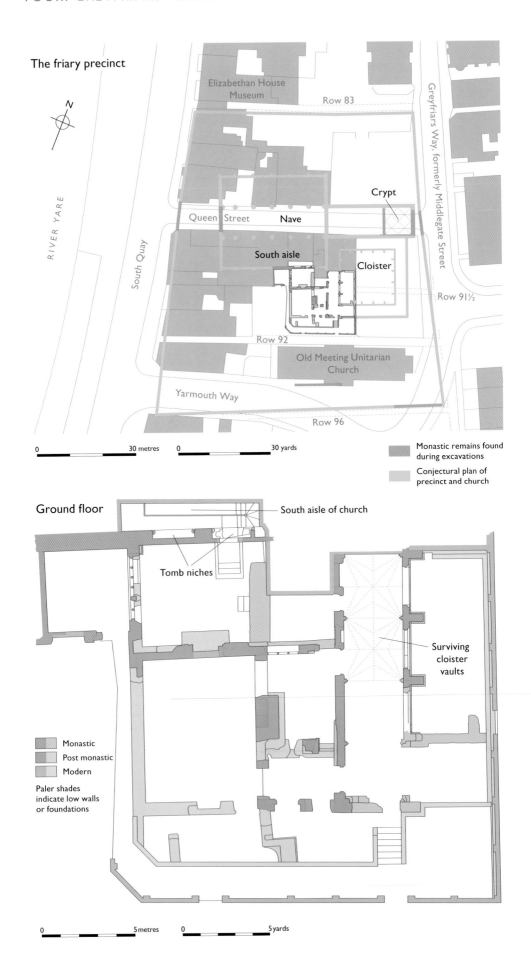

The friary precinct

RIVER YARE

South Quay

Elizabethan House Museum

Row 83

Greyfriars' Way, formerly Middlegate Street

Crypt

Queen Street   Nave

South aisle

Cloister

Row 91½

Row 92

Old Meeting Unitarian Church

Yarmouth Way

Row 96

0 ——— 30 metres   0 ——— 30 yards

Monastic remains found during excavations

Conjectural plan of precinct and church

Ground floor

South aisle of church

Tomb niches

Surviving cloister vaults

Monastic

Post monastic

Modern

Paler shades indicate low walls or foundations

0 ——— 5 metres   0 ——— 5 yards

GREYFRIARS' CLOISTER

The Franciscan friars or Friars Minor – popularly known as the grey friars in England, from the colour of their habits – were established in Great Yarmouth by the early 1270s and probably decades earlier. At its full extent the friary occupied a large area from the river on the west side to Middlegate Street to the east, and from Row 83 on the north side to Row 96 on the south. The length of the church, which was under construction in 1291, suggests that it was among the largest Franciscan churches in the country, a reflection of Yarmouth's great wealth at the time.

The friary was suppressed by Henry VIII in 1538 and granted to Thomas Cromwell and his nephew Sir Richard Williams, after which it changed hands several times until it was passed to various members of the town assembly in 1569. The church was demolished and the stone used to build the new Broad Row, now Queen Street, on its site. The church ran much the length of the new street, which follows the line of the nave. Some of the conventual buildings were incorporated into houses, and by the end of the 19th century the remains of the cloister were to be found in cottages in Row 91½. In 1887 the Tolhouse Trustees (see page 38) acquired the cottages so that visitors could view the cloister.

The cottages were bombed in 1942 and the surrounding buildings destroyed. Only a few walls were left standing, exposing 16th- and 17th-century doors and fireplaces – and the south-western part of the cloister. The visitor today is confronted with a jumble of buildings representing the remains of the cloister and buildings erected on the site after the friary was suppressed. The standing remains of the friary itself are now difficult to interpret.

Cloister

The cloister was an open court surrounded by covered walkways which lay immediately south of the church. It originally formed a square and extended north and east beyond the modern wall to the site of the car park. The one reference we have to the cloister before the suppression is to the bailiffs often holding their courts here. This is perhaps less surprising than it sounds: living as they did in the heart of towns, friars were highly accessible to the local population and there are references to them being used as mediators in disputes within other towns.

The four surviving bays were part of the west walkway of the 14th-century cloister. The two northern bays retain their decorative vaulting, each with a carved boss at the main intersections. A two-bay chamber to the west, also vaulted, contains the remains of a 16th-century fireplace. The walls of the surviving cloister walk are faced with a mixture of bricks and broken flints. The stone wall arches and ribs spring from

Above: Decorative rib vaulting in the north-western corner of the cloister, with carved bosses at the rib intersections
Below: A drawing of a Franciscan friar, from a 15th-century version of William Langland's Piers Plowman. Langland criticized the friars for their alleged vices

Facing page: Plan of Greyfriars' Cloister, showing conjectural plan of the friary and the extent of its precinct superimposed on a modern map of the town (top), and the surviving remains (bottom)

Above: The remains of the cloister seen from the south-east. The room above the vaulted cloister walk was used as a school in the 19th century

Below: Detail from a window inserted into a first-floor chamber on the Greyfriars site after the friary's suppression in 1538

triple shafts with moulded capitals. The bases end 45cm above the ground, because they were designed to spring from a bench that ran along the cloister walk.

The large door in the second bay from the north gave access to a vaulted staircase that rose alongside the west wall of the cloister to a two-bay vaulted landing on the first floor. This connected the galleries above the cloister walks to a room to the west. In the 19th century, the room above the cloister was used as a school. After the suppression in 1538 the conventual buildings were adapted for domestic use, and fireplaces and timber window frames were inserted, the remains of which can be seen on the site.

Church

The early friars lived in small groups in ordinary town houses, but as the success of their mission grew, they began to build churches and conventual buildings resembling monasteries. By the late 13th century friary churches were being built all over Europe. They were distinctive in that they were designed to accommodate large numbers of people who came to listen to the friars' sermons, and also had more altars at which to celebrate Mass than all but the largest parish churches. We know that the grey friars' church at Yarmouth was being built in 1291 as a prominent burgess, Oliver Wyth, left 40 marks in his will for the raising of the gable (see page 29).

The antiquary John Ives (d.1776) noted 'an ancient stone coffin' built into a wall here which supposedly contained the bones of the founder. He does not specify where this was, but it is possible that he was referring to a tomb that once stood in one of the elaborate recesses in what was the south wall of the church's south aisle. These were discovered during building work in the 1960s. A door has been hacked through the eastern recess, and the back of the fireplace visible from outside protrudes into the arches, which originally would have extended all the way down the nave. Nevertheless, two limestone canopies survive almost intact, and there are remains of a third. The tomb slab and fragmentary slender colonettes in the recesses are carved from Purbeck marble.

On the back wall of the west tomb recess are the remains of a wall-painting, which though now faded and fragmentary is of the highest quality and is dated to about 1310. A female figure wearing a widow's headdress with white veil (possibly St Anne) is seen within an elaborate architectural framework. The most expensive and brilliant colours were used for the painting: azurite for blue, vermilion red, bright copper greens and a liberal use of gold. Many people were keen to be buried in friary churches, and so contributed towards the cost of a church and its decoration, much to the annoyance of the local parish which lost out on revenue (see page 30).

Other Friary Buildings

Although we know where the cloister and church stood (the location of the latter, together with the precinct walls to east and west, was discovered during the construction of a sewer in 1896), we can only build up a general picture of the other buildings and the precinct as there is little specific documentation. Small clues come from the years following the friary's suppression. We know there was a 'mulberry tree', because in 1572 the corporation ordered it to be sold for 4 shillings. In 1599 'the orchard' was rented out. The 'Green Yard' of the friary was later used as an exercise yard by the Trained Bands (local militias), and in 1636 a house there was pulled down to enlarge the space.

In 1581–2 Thomas Damet leased part of the buildings 'from the entry by the old parlour to the northward and eastward with the gardens and bleaching place, the long entry with the court and kitchen yards', on condition that when a 'man of honour' visited the town, he would be able to lodge there. The friars had probably kept a guest house: in a busy port there would have been a demand both for lodgings and for the friars to hear the confessions of foreign merchants visiting the herring fair, or of people embarking on pilgrimage to and from the Continent. Margery Kempe of King's Lynn made an offering before an image of the Virgin Mary at Yarmouth before setting sail on her pilgrimage to the Holy Land in 1413.

'And I shal covere your kirk, youre cloistre do maken, Wowes [walls] do whiten and wyndowes glazen, Do peynten and portraye who paied for the makyng' (William Langland, in Piers Plowman, III: 60–63), *describing how rich patrons funded the elaborate decoration found in friaries. The painting at Greyfriars' church (detail above) must have been commissioned by someone of great wealth, as the work and materials used are of the finest quality*

Gesaltzen fisch.

History

Great Yarmouth's
remarkable situation,
on a narrow sand spit
bounded by the river
Yare on one side and
the North Sea on the
other, explains much of
its singular history and
development. Living
on a quasi-island, its
inhabitants displayed
the characteristics of
islanders: fiercely proud
and independent, they
were great seafarers
and traders, especially
with Holland. The town
drew its wealth from the
sea, most famously from
herring. The network of
narrow lanes, or rows,
confined within its walls,
survived largely intact
into the 20th century,
a characteristic of the
town and a curiosity
to visitors.

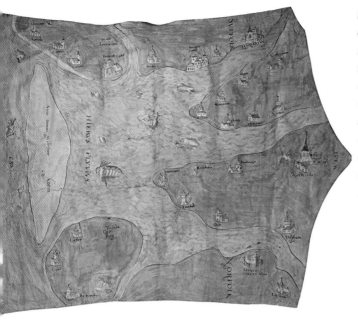

EARLY HISTORY

Great Yarmouth sits on a narrow sand spit at the mouth of the river Yare. In Roman times the land where the town now stands was still under water – part of the 'Great Estuary' which commanded access to Norfolk's rivers and was vital for shipping the county's riches to the Continent. The Romans built forts at Caister-on-Sea and Burgh to defend the estuary, which were part of the 'Saxon Shore' chain of defence along England's south and east coast. This guarded against attack from the Saxons and other peoples from northern Europe, who began to harass England's coast from about AD 200.

By the time Roman rule ended in Britain at the beginning of the 5th century, the sea level had begun to fall. The mouth of the estuary gradually became blocked by a sandbank, which grew steadily south from Caister and by the 11th century was linked to the mainland to the north. Great Yarmouth – the mouth of the river Yare – is built on this sandbank. At first it was colonized by seasonal fishermen, but by the time of the Domesday survey in 1086 it was a royal borough attached to the neighbouring manor of Gorleston, with a chapel dedicated to St Benet, 70 burgesses and 24 fishermen.

The first inhabitants seem to have settled on the highest area of the spit, at its northern end, called Fullers Hill, or 'le Howe' (the hill). By 1200 the spit had greatly expanded towards the south, although it remained narrow. The main north–south thoroughfares through the town may represent successive shorelines as it expanded westwards, and the singular, confined layout of the town may be due to the fact that the spit was so much narrower in the Middle Ages. The spit later expanded eastwards towards the sea but this area, the Den, or Denes, remained largely undeveloped until the 19th century.

Map of Great Yarmouth
in about 1585

A South Gate (14th century)

B Blackfriars (built 1271)

C Tolhouse (12th century)

D Castle (pre-1208)

E Greyfriars (c.1271)

F Whitefriars (c.1278)

G North Gate (14th century)

H St Nicholas's church and priory
(1101)

I St Mary's hospital (c.1278)

J Marketplace (note the cross
and pillory, 1395)

K Crane (1528)

L South Mount (1569)

M The Denes

N River Yare

O Breydon Water

Medieval thoroughfares

P Foreland

Q The Conge

R The Howe

S Northgate

T Little, or Blind, Middlegate

U Great Middlegate

*Below: The Tolhouse in the 1860s, with
a troll cart or harry carry, specially
designed for Yarmouth's narrow rows,
passing by. Gutted in the Second
World War, the Tolhouse has since
been restored and is now a museum*

THE MEDIEVAL TOWN

Great Yarmouth was a boom town in the 13th century,
almost doubling in size by expansion onto its former quays.
When assessed for tax in 1334 it ranked as the fourth richest
provincial town in England. A 16th-century map of Yarmouth
(see above), although it dates from after the Suppression of the
Monasteries (note that Greyfriars' church is roofless), gives a
good impression of the medieval town. Even today, several
medieval structures remain, including the town wall, which is
among the best preserved in England. Large sections of it
survive, including 11 towers, seven of which are largely intact.
Henry III granted permission for the walls to be built in 1261,
although work did not begin until 1285, and continued through
the 14th century. The main purpose was defensive, but the
walls also served as a customs barrier, to ensure that tolls were
paid and traders regulated.

The walls surrounded the town on three sides, the river
forming a natural defence and boundary on the western side.
The town's eastern side was defined by the Denes, which was
used for drying nets and as pasture for the town's animals. The
long, narrow town was divided laterally into four 'leets' and the
local administration of the town was based on these divisions.
Each leet seems to have had a windmill associated with it,
which stood on the Denes.

A castle, described as the 'kinges ston hus', stood between
Rows 99 and 101, at the end of Howard Street. Built before
1208, it probably stood at what was the early southernmost

limit of the town. It was ruinous by the early 17th century, and no trace of it remains. By contrast, the nearby 12th-century Tolhouse is a remarkable survival. Originally a merchant's house, it was in civic use by the late 13th century. The remains of an equally substantial house of similar date survive in the form of a 12th-century barrel-vaulted chamber beneath Nos 50–56 Howard Street South.

At the heart of the medieval town was the priory church of St Nicholas, which also served the parish. Founded in 1101 by the bishop of Norwich, the priory was run by a group of Benedictine monks as a cell of Norwich Cathedral Priory. The church was badly bombed during the Second World War but restored afterwards. A 14th-century hall attached to it, now part of a school, survives. To the south of the church were the guildhall, where the town's ruling assembly met, and the enormous marketplace. It is likely that the annual herring fair was held in the huge open space to its south, which ran the length of the town. The market cross lay at its centre: this was where the pillory and stocks stood, and where punishments such as whipping took place. The last market cross was pulled down in 1835, and its site is now marked by a plaque.

In the 13th century fish curing seems to have been centred at the Howe (Fuller's Hill), near the Conge, from where supplies of salt were possibly obtained. Near the North Gate was Gropecuntlane, presumably the 13th-century red light district. Two leper houses lay outside this gate; they were later used as 'pesthouses' for plague victims.

Below: The south-east tower of the town wall in 1865. Large sections of the medieval wall survive, including 11 towers, and a stretch of wall north of the south-east tower retains its battlements. The distinctive flint and brick work on the upper parts of the tower dates from a rebuilding in the early 16th century, probably to accommodate cannon

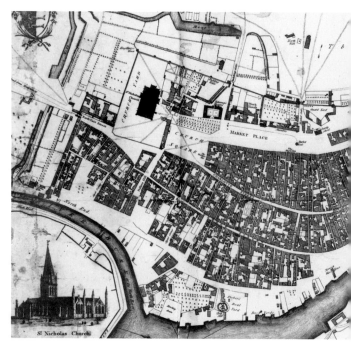

St Nicholas Church

'Many and many a
picturesque old bit of
domestic architecture is to
be hunted amongst the
rows. In some rows … the
houses retreat into tiny
courts, where washing and
clear-starching are done …'
From a description of the
rows in Household Words
(1853), possibly by Charles
Dickens (above), who visited
Great Yarmouth in 1849
(see page 36) and thought
it 'the strangest place in all
the wide world'

THE ROWS

By the late 13th century there were three main streets running
north–south across the town: Northgate, Southgate and
Middlegate. Long, narrow blocks of property running back from
the streets east–west, which equated to burgage plots, were
first mentioned in the mid-12th century. They were known as
'rengia' (range) or 'rengata'. The earliest archaeological
evidence for their existence dates to about the same time.
The rows themselves were the lanes separating the rengia.

The earliest use of the word 'row' occurs in Yarmouth in the
early 1280s in 'le spitalrowe' (hospital row). The rows are also
described as horse and foot passages at about this time. Until
1804 they were not numbered but known by the name of the
person whose house fronted the row: so, for example, Row
117 was known as Josh Peartree's for a time. A manuscript of
1286 lists 99 rows, but as the section describing the north of
the town is lost, there were presumably many more in total.
Thomas Nashe in his *Lenten Stuffe* of 1599 speaks of 'lanes
seven score' (140), the same number given by Henry Manship,
who completed a history of the town in 1619. Although the
number of rows varies depending on whether half rows
(cul-de-sacs) or new rows laid out after the Suppression of the
Monasteries are counted, 145 is the usually accepted number.

While many medieval towns had narrow alleyways, or
rows, leading off the main streets between properties, they
existed to a remarkably complete extent in Yarmouth, almost
forming a grid pattern. Many explanations have been given for
this, including as a means of defence against floods, war and
weather. A more likely reason is the constricted nature of the
site and its expansion towards a westward-shifting river bank.

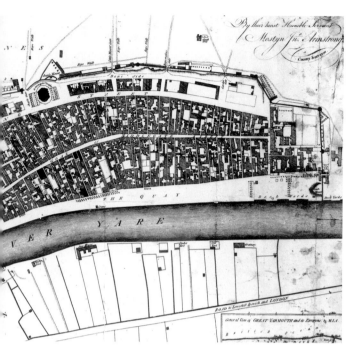

THE GREY FRIARS

The establishment of the friars in Yarmouth in the 13th century
is an indication of the town's prosperity, for as a mendicant or
begging order they were dependent on donations to fund
them and their churches. The town was evidently prosperous
enough to sustain friars of four different orders – Franciscans,
Carmelites, Austins and Dominicans.

The Friars Minor or Minorites, also known as Franciscans
after their founder, St Francis of Assisi, and as the grey friars
because of their grey habit, were settled in Norwich in 1226.
They are thought to have come to Yarmouth soon after,
although the friary is first mentioned only in 1271, when it was
licensed to enclose and build over a lane on the north side
of the friary church on the town's land. This was by order of
Henry III on the advice of his son, Edward, who had observed
'the narrowness of the place' where the friars were lodged: a
reference perhaps to the friars being housed in a row.

The friary extended its precinct by acquiring property
piecemeal through a series of bequests. In 1285, for example,
the friars were allowed to extend over a row adjoining their
precinct provided that the row be left 'open and common' so
that Thomas Gerbrigge [Gerberge], whose father had left them
the land, should retain access to his property there. In 1290
John, son of Nicholas de Bromholm, gave them land lying
between the precinct to the north and a common lane on the
south side (Row 96). The prominent merchant Oliver Wyth
left 40 marks in his will of 1291 for raising the church gable.

The friars continued to acquire property following the Black
Death. In 1356 Thomas de Drayton gave them 'three void
places', 100 feet (30m) wide and 250 feet (76m) long, on the

Above: A carved head from Greyfriars' Cloister

Below: Part of the cloister at Greyfriars. After the suppression of the friary in 1538, the precinct fell into various hands; the town used part of it as a guest house for important visitors, and other buildings were converted into private dwellings or demolished

north side of the friary, with the provision that they repaired and built the Quay when necessary. In return they were allowed an 'easement' on the Quay 'to store, bring and take away victuals and other necessaries'.

The friars attracted recruits from noteworthy families in the town. William atte Mawe, town bailiff in 1354, directed his body to be buried in the church and his estate to be sold to pay for the celebration of masses and alms for the repose of his soul at the discretion of his nephew, Thomas Sond, who was a friar there. Almost the last we hear of the Yarmouth grey friars before the suppression is of a friar called John Rokeby, who weighed 24 stone – a fact considered so remarkable that it justified an entry on the Borough Roll in 1492.

The friars were not universally revered. A commission was set up in 1302 to investigate the friars' allegation that vandals had broken the pavement near their wall so that rainwater was running under it, and that 'some of the townsmen with strangers' had destroyed the hedge which they had made as a defence 'against the flow and violence of the sea' by putting timber and heavy weights on it. Their success in attracting burials and bequests, which were a lucrative business, also set them at odds with the established church. In 1484 the prior of Yarmouth brought complaints against them to the bishop of Norwich 'for unlawfully burying three men killed in the ship of our Lord the King'. He felt so strongly that he spent 10s. 5d. in hiring horses for three journeys to Norwich to pursue his claim.

YARMOUTH IN THE SIXTEENTH CENTURY

By the early 16th century Yarmouth had fallen from ranking fourth among provincial towns in England to twentieth. The silting up of the harbour in the 1340s, a reduction in the number of herring caught off its shores and the death of many inhabitants in the Black Death of 1349 had had a severe impact on the town. It is likely that the friars, who moved freely among the population, hearing confession, ministering to the sick and burying the dead, were badly hit by the plague. In 1502 the burgesses reported that after the Black Death 'the moste parte of the dwelying places and inhabitacions of the said towne stode desolate and fell into utter ruyn and decay which at this day are gardeyns and voide groundes'. Nevertheless, the duke of Norfolk, visiting in 1545, found it 'the properest towne, the best buylded with most substancyall houses, that I know so near the sea in all your Majesties' realme'.

Greyfriars was suppressed by Henry VIII in 1538 and granted to Thomas Cromwell and his nephew Sir Richard Williams. It changed hands several times over the following decades, and parts were sold off to various people. The town was swift to take what advantage it could. Any former property of defunct religious institutions that had been leased out and neglected was seized, and in 1546 any remaining

assets were put to the use of the parish church, the harbour and the town fortifications.

Descriptions of Yarmouth from this period paint a picture of small houses, densely built, with courtyards, gardens and shared facilities such as wells. 'Two chambers and two gardens' were leased to a priest and tailor; the latter, John Rogerson, and his wife, Beatrice, were instructed to keep the roof of their house wind and watertight and to keep it in repair. Some common land was enclosed during this period. As in later times, wells were often shared with neighbours: Christopher Sylle, yeoman, had the right to draw water at the well in Nicholas Heyth's yard, provided that he paid towards its upkeep and did 'not annoy the said Nicholas by reason of the window opening towards the well'. One indication that living conditions were overcrowded is found in the regulations regarding the grazing and keeping of animals: the number of cows per household was restricted, bullocks and sheep were forbidden, and inhabitants could not feed their animals in front of their doors due to the 'inordynat number of neate [cattle] kept within this town to the great noyance of the same'.

By 1549 the harbour had silted up to such an extent that ships had to be drawn across the Denes with capstans or unloaded in the roads or on the beach. In 1566 the problem was at last solved by a Dutch engineer, Joas Johnson, who built the seventh (and final) haven, as the entrance to the harbour was known.

Above: The South Gate, Great Yarmouth, *by John Sell Cotman, who lived in the town from 1811 to 1823. The medieval gate was demolished in 1812*

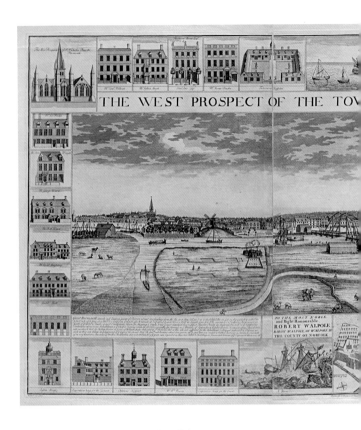

THE WEST PROSPECT OF THE TOW

Below: Row III House was one of many houses built of brick and flint after the town banned building in wood in 1571. The next 40 years saw a housing boom as the town increased in size and prosperity

REBUILDING THE TOWN

In 1571 the town imposed a ban on building in wood and reed thatch as a fire precaution. This coincided with a precipitous rise in the town's fortunes, which Henry Manship put down to the success of the seventh haven and the return of herring to Yarmouth in the summer. Writing in 1612–19, he observed that in the preceding 40 years Yarmouth was 'in more than a fourth part in the buildings augmented and in the number of inhabitants increased'. Houses were now built of brick and flint and roofed with tiles. The Old Merchant's House and Row III House were among those built during this period of rapid change: by 1629 there were 1,200 households in the town.

Yarmouth had long-standing trading and cultural links with the Low Countries. In 1570, 70 refugee 'Flemings' were granted leave to settle here. The Dutch were given the use of part of the Town House as their chapel in the early 17th century, of which one wall remains, marked by a plaque. Dutch building styles had a strong influence in the town.

Heavy bombing during the Second World War uncovered a large concentration of early 17th-century buildings within the rows area. The majority seem to have been small units, with one room on each floor and a basement accessible only from outside, but built in larger blocks. There were also more considerable dwellings to be found, such as the Old Merchant's House and Row III House. Medieval foundations were discovered beneath the cobbled yard at the north of Row III House and the house's foundations represent the lower

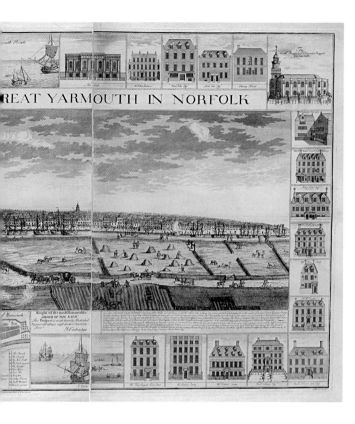

GREAT YARMOUTH IN NORFOLK

Left: 'No maritime town in England is better provided with fine houses than Yarmouth' wrote Henry Manship in his history of the town in 1619. This 1724 engraving, The West Prospect of the Town of Great Yarmouth in Norfolk, by John Harris (fl. 1686–1740) after J Corbridge, shows some of the finest buildings of the town in the margins

Left: 'No maritime town in England is better provided with fine houses than Yarmouth' wrote Henry Manship in his history of the town in 1619. This 1724 engraving, The West Prospect of the Town of Great Yarmouth in Norfolk, by John Harris (fl. 1686–1740) after J Corbridge, shows some of the finest buildings of the town in the margins

Below: Some of the decorative brickwork once found in the rows. The wall surrounding the yard of Row 111 House contains different examples of typical brick and flint patterns

parts of an earlier building, probably built in the latter part of the 16th century.

Timber-framed houses did not simply disappear overnight, of course. Some houses were built onto and incorporated earlier chimney-stacks, these being the only part of houses not made of wood. There is evidence to suggest that the east range of Row III House could once have had a timber-framed structure adjoining it on its east side.

Glimpses of an expanding town trying to exist within a confined space appear in the town records. In 1618 it was decreed that all doors opening outwards into the rows should be made to swing inwards, 'otherwise the constables would nail them up and levy a fine of 5s. on owners'. In 1622 the number of taverns, or 'tippling houses' as they were called, was increased to 40 and restricted at that number.

The mid-17th century was a period of turmoil for Great Yarmouth and the country as a whole: this was the time of the Civil Wars, when Yarmouth came out for Parliament, and then of the Anglo-Dutch wars, which naturally affected the town because of its many trading links with Holland. In 1655 Yarmouth found its finances under huge strain for maintaining the haven and piers and from great losses sustained at sea from pirates and enemy ships. The Greyfriars site was valued and in January 1657 sold off to John Woodroffe for £2,600 on condition that he should build a broad row and a narrow row on the premises, 'according to a plan made therof'. This New Broad Row is now Queen Street.

Right: An 18th-century French engraving of a herring smokehouse. The herring trade supported many subsidiary ones, such as basket making (Yarmouth had distinctively shaped baskets called swills), box making and net mending
Below: Scottish 'herring girls' on the Quay in 1947. The women came down from Scotland in their hundreds to gut and pack fish during the herring season (see page 38)

'Silver Darlings'

'There is yearly in September the worthiest herring fishery in Europe which draweth great concourse of people, which maketh the town much the richer ... but very unsavoury for the time'

Great Yarmouth built its wealth on herring, the 'silver darlings' which arrived in great shoals off the Norfolk coast to feed every autumn. In the days before refrigeration, herring, which kept well when salted or smoked, were an important part of the medieval and early modern diet. In the medieval period it was consumed by all members of society: Yarmouth herring supplied the royal household, the army and the monasteries, where meat was generally forbidden.

When the autumn shoals appeared, large numbers of fishermen and merchants flocked to the great 'Free Herring Fair', held over the 40 days from Michaelmas to Martinmas. As John Speed wrote in 1611, 'There is yearly in September the worthiest herring fishery in Europe which draweth great concourse of people, which maketh the town much the richer all the year following but very unsavoury for the time.' Great Yarmouth guarded its lucrative trade jealously and did everything it could to acquire and maintain a monopoly. In the Middle Ages the powerful Cinque Ports on the south coast held the right to administer justice during the Herring Fair, causing resentment which sometimes spilled into violence: in 1297, for instance, men of the Cinque Ports attacked Yarmouth ships in the English fleet and many ships were lost. Eventually Yarmouth was given joint administration over the fair, although Cinque Port bailiffs continued to visit ceremonially until 1662.

A large proportion of the red herring cured in Yarmouth was sent to Rotterdam, from where it was despatched throughout Europe. Ships also sailed directly to the Mediterranean; by the 19th century Italy was the chief export market for red herring.

EIGHTEENTH-CENTURY PROSPERITY

Shortly after John Andrews, known as 'the greatest herring merchant in Europe', had built his palatial new house on the quayside, now 20 South Quay, Daniel Defoe described Yarmouth's quay as 'the finest in England, if not in Europe'. All sorts of new goods were being imported into Britain from an ever-increasing number of colonies and Yarmouth's marketplace was amply stocked with them. In 1697 the town had over one thousand ships. In addition to the herring fleet, sailing ships exported vast quantities of herring to Holland, Italy, Spain and Portugal, alongside Norwich cloth. There was also a flourishing trade with Norway and the Baltic, from which came timber, hemp, flax and sailcloth. Yarmouth ships fished for cod further afield and, later in the century, engaged in whaling.

Many houses were adapted to keep up with changing fashions: mullion windows were replaced by sashes in the late 17th and early 18th centuries, panelling was painted, and buffet cupboards (see page 8) were installed to display fashionable tea-drinking paraphernalia and the gentility of the inhabitants.

Defoe observed that the rows made Great Yarmouth 'the most regular built town in England ... and seems to have been built all at once; or that the dimensions of the houses, and extent of the streets were laid out by consent', although he also noted one defect of this most prosperous town – there was little room to accommodate the expanding population.

In 1759 sea baths opened near the beach and Yarmouth began to develop as a seaside resort as well as a port; the town began to spread from the river towards the sea. The row houses saw a decline in status and by the turn of the century the Old Merchant's House had been divided into two.

'The women stood in their doors, some with both hands full of dirt and others with bowls full of water, which they threw at me as I passed by'
Despite a long tradition of Nonconformism in Yarmouth, Thomas Olivers (above), the first Methodist to preach there in 1754, was ill received in the rows

Below: The Fishermen's Hospital, 1702, with its distinctive Dutch gable. The original cartouche ornament is on display at the Old Merchant's House

Above: The Dutch Fair at Great Yarmouth, *by George Vincent, 1821. The Britannia Monument to the left was erected in honour of Nelson in 1817–19. Trade with Holland was badly affected by the Napoleonic wars and operated on a much reduced scale after 1815*

Below: Peggotty and Little Emily, *characters from Charles Dickens's* David Copperfield, *sitting outside their upturned boat house on Yarmouth beach. Dickens was much taken by Great Yarmouth and wrote the novel after his brief visit there*

VICTORIAN GREAT YARMOUTH

In the late 1840s, the 72-year-old Dawson Turner (who saved the merchant-mark wall anchor now on display at the Old Merchant's House – see page 1) commented on how few of the houses in the early 18th-century map drawn by Corbridge (pages 32–3) were recognizable and how every house on the Quay had undergone extensive alterations in his lifetime. He lamented the loss of 'the porches attached to the doors, those comfortable summer-evening lounges, in which the father dreamed over his pipe or paper, while his family sat round him, chatting with and of the passers by'.

Soon after Turner wrote this, Charles Dickens briefly visited Yarmouth in January 1849. He concluded that it was 'the strangest place in the wide world' and returned to London with the inspiration for the 'spongy world' of Peggotty and his upturned boat in his novel *David Copperfield*. The town may have seemed quaint to an outsider, but it was changing rapidly. It was first lit by gas in 1824. By the mid-1850s there were waterworks, new houses along the beach, an esplanade, a public hospital, national schools, a poor house, churches of all denominations, steam flour mills, a corn hall, a new fish market, improvements to the harbour and two new piers. By 1870 the resort was attracting about 78,000 summer visitors, 63,000 coming by rail and 15,000 by passenger steamer.

The herring were now distributed round the country by rail – more than half of them to London – and thousands of barrels were also transported by steamer. The rows became ever more densely built up and the process of subdividing houses to let continued.

Life in the Rows

In the early years of the 19th century, the Old Merchant's House was owned by Robert Cory, who was mayor of Great Yarmouth in 1803. His son, Robert Cory junior, also a prominent townsman and mayor, lived in a large house in Row 76. In 1814 he hosted a table at the end of his row at a dinner to celebrate Napoleon's defeat. Tables were placed the entire length of the Quay and guests were treated to hot roast beef, plum pudding and ale, with tobacco for the men and snuff for the elderly ladies. The day concluded with a bonfire, pig hunts and donkey races.

After the Corys sold the house it passed through a series of landlords. By 1851, and probably much earlier, the house had been divided into two separate cottages. At this date Simon Fleet, a fish merchant, and his wife, a beetster or net-braider, shared the east half (later No. 9) with William Parsons, a keelman. In the early 1870s this was occupied as one tenement by Edward James Self, a tailor, his wife, Hannah, and their four children. George Small, a musician, and his wife, Elizabeth, lived in the west part with their stepson. By the 1890s, a clearly impoverished household at No. 8 consisted of Martha King, a widowed tailoress, her young son, her 84-year-old mother, described in the 1891 census as a pauper, and two single female lodgers, one of whom was also a pauper.

Many families in the rows sublet their houses, taking lodgers. In the 1930s the Lees, who lived in the east wing of Row 111 House, took in guests from London during the summer season. Space was limited: even without guests, the two girls shared a bedroom with their parents, while the two boys slept in a tiny alcove. Nonetheless, Raymond Lee, who was a boy at the time, recalls the guests with pleasure because, thrillingly, they had a car.

Surrounding the houses by the end of the 19th century were malthouses, smokehouses and factories. Raymond Lee recalls not just the pungent smell but also the constant sounds heard through flimsy partition walls, and the clack of clogs on cobblestones from the streets outside. Alan Morris, who was born in Row 3, remembers vividly the rats scurrying across the roofs, despite the inhabitants' best efforts to keep their houses clean.

Guests were treated to hot roast beef, plum pudding and ale, with snuff for the elderly ladies

Above: Joshua Lee (centre), who lived in the east wing of Row 111 House in the 1930s, with a group of Great Yarmouth fishermen

Below: A feast held for over 8,000 people at Great Yarmouth on 19 April 1814 to celebrate Napoleon's abdication. Robert Cory, whose family owned the Old Merchant's House at the time, is at the head of the table. The engraving is by John Sell Cotman, who was then living in the town

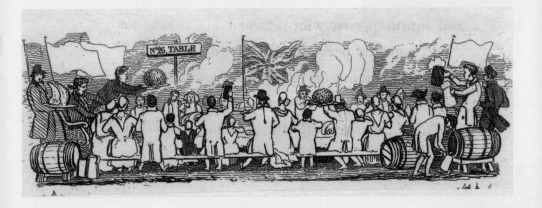

Above: The Empire Cinema, on Marine Parade, which opened in 1911, was one of six cinemas built in Yarmouth in the early 20th century – a reflection of the town's booming population as well as its popularity as a resort

THE TWENTIETH CENTURY

At the end of the 19th century the Old Merchant's House was owned by Caroline Emma Benton, the wife of a porter of Peterhouse, Cambridge. She rented it out as Nos 8 and 9 Row 117. In 1908 No. 8 was acquired at auction by Great Yarmouth Historical Buildings, successor to the Tolhouse Trustees as the body responsible for restoring the Tolhouse (see page 27) and preserving Greyfriars' Cloister; it acquired the latter (by buying the cottages that contained it) in 1906. It opened them to visitors and gave No. 8, Row 117 a new tenant; the public could view the ceilings for a small charge. In the summer of 1913, a record summer for the Great Yarmouth fishing industry, over 3,000 people visited Greyfriars' Cloister.

The following year, the declaration of war in August saw an exodus of visitors and a premature end to the season. German ships bombarded Yarmouth, which achieved the dubious accolade of being the first place in Britain to be hit by a Zeppelin. Greyfriars' Cloister remained shut, and in the slump that followed the war the trustees reported that unemployment had meant that it was 'impossible to collect the rents closely'.

The Threat of Demolition

In 1926 the Ancient Monuments Board of England made the Old Merchant's House and Greyfriars' Cloister scheduled monuments. Soon after, however, many of the row houses were threatened with demolition. In January 1933, the town council declared the area between Rows 17 and 21 to the north and the midline of Rows 28 and 27 to the south a clearance area, and made a compulsory purchase order. This affected 135 houses accommodating some 144 families and a population of 600. The council proposed to move the

'By October the fisher girls had arrived. We usually had four girls who shared a bedroom. They brought most things with them, including a sack of potatoes. They worked all day, and sometimes in the evenings, with flares for lighting, three girls gutting and one packing. Layers of fish, tails to the middle of the barrel, a layer of salt, then more fish, till it was filled.

'They worked with bare arms and always had a shawl and wellie boots, and an overskirt of oilskin with a bib. They did their fingers up in rags tied with cotton. When they came home there were pails of water in the yard to wash their hands. The aprons were stood up in the yard, with their boots.

'The girls used to buy lots of goods to take home. There was a special train for them to travel back in – it took the best part of two days.'

Audrey Ward recalls the fisher girls who lodged with her family in the 1950s; (left) Scots fisher girls knitting on the quayside in the early 20th century

inhabitants to an estate in Gorleston. Needless to say, this was hugely controversial, both among residents worried about being moved out of town, and among business owners and landlords concerned that they would be inadequately compensated. While many people did live in cramped, damp, dilapidated houses, with shared external taps and lavatories, and were keen to leave, others lived in larger houses, with many more rooms than they would be offered if they moved.

After the order had been given, an atmosphere of uncertainty prevailed. In January 1936 a report issued by the Society for the Protection of Ancient Buildings and the Norfolk and Norwich Archaeological Society conceded that some areas of the rows should be replanned, but proposed that just under a third be preserved. The clearance plans, however, were soon overtaken by events.

THE SECOND WORLD WAR AND AFTER

During the Second World War, Great Yarmouth suffered intense bombing. The town's streets were deserted of visitors, all the beaches were mined and every road leading to the sea front had barricades of herring barrels. Children were evacuated, invasion was expected daily from the summer of 1940 into 1941, and the town's inhabitants prepared to evacuate at a moment's notice. At one point they were instructed to slaughter all domestic fowl and rabbits. In 1941 there were 167 raids, with over 7,000 incendiary bombs and 803 high explosives dropped. The area that received the greatest damage was that of the rows between South Quay and Middlegate Street. In a strange echo from the 17th century, the area around Greyfriars became a training ground for soldiers once more.

Below: The remains of Greyfriars' Cloister and neighbouring cottages in 1942, after Second World War bombing had destroyed two of the four remaining cloister bays

Above: South Quay in 2008

Below: Market Row, one of the few remaining rows in Great Yarmouth, seen from the south-west today

Even as the bombs fell, the town planning officer, K K Parker, published a report in June 1943 which concluded that where a building would obstruct a clearance scheme, it should be demolished. Greyfriars, he wrote, had been so badly damaged that 'its retention is not worth while': a plaque indicating the site would, he felt, retain the connection. He prescribed the same fate for the Elizabethan House on South Quay, which in the event was bequeathed to the National Trust in 1943 and escaped destruction.

At one point there were discussions to see if the Old Merchant's House could be incorporated in some way with the adjoining pub. In May 1947, however, the Office of Works was asked to take over the running of the cloister and the Old Merchant's House, and in 1954 the latter was opened as a museum displaying wall anchors and other items salvaged from the rows area.

Meanwhile Row III House was also restored and opened to the public in the 1950s. The Great Yarmouth Preservation Trust, successor to Great Yarmouth Historical Buildings, is still active: in 2001 it purchased and renovated the Nelson Museum at 26 South Quay, opposite Row III House.

By the 1950s, most of the rows had gone and the herring industry too was dying. With them went the intensity of sounds and smell of a busy port whose inhabitants had, for most of its history, lived as closely packed as the barrels of herring which were their livelihood. Row III House and the Old Merchant's House survive as witnesses of this vanished way of life and of a type of building almost entirely lost.